THE FIRST 9 YEARS ON THE LD HIGHWAY

A Mother's story and Her Son's journey...

Written by DA2

PublishAmerica
Baltimore

First printing

PublishAmerica has allowed this work to remain exactly as the author intended, verbatim, without editorial input.

Softcover 9781413765151
PUBLISHED BY PUBLISHAMERICA, LLLP
www.publishamerica.com
Baltimore

Printed in the United States of America

Ignorance or Personal Disbelief in Learning Differences / Disabilities puts up a wall between you and the world of amazing little thinkers and adapters. "They who look at a glass, as in both being halfway full and halfway empty"

—DA2

To My

Children and their children's Children
and All of you I don't know.

*"Somewhere beyond the doubt, there's a shiny part of you,
waiting to be discovered...don't ever stop looking"*

—DA2

Thank you G.

IF YOU'RE HOLDING THIS BOOK chances are; you, your child or that someone you know, has Learning Differences / Disabilities also known as a Neurobiological Disorder. *"An Ingenious, Contradictory and Chameleonic Disorder,"*...That can hide among our children's natural intelligences and their marvelous innocent splendor, hindering their self-worth to grow. It can cleverly disguise itself into something it may truly not be. *LD* has the cunning ability to become an unidentifiable shameful secrete that manipulates our children's thoughts about themselves, as they quietly hide It away from the people who surround them. *LD* can manifest its self among them as a behavioral and or a discipline issue, therefore miserably being mistaken and misunderstood as one, if not examined thoroughly without fear or prejudice. *LD*, can be exceptionally difficult to detect by our children's outer appearances, unless you have a close personal connection or knowledge of the subtle signs that come with It. *"It may take being one, to know one, to recognize it"*...This disorder, if it's allowed, has all the ability to invisibly pull our children apart from the inside out, as they become prisoners of themselves, unable to find their identity and true value as a productive little person in their world. The similarities and differences of this complex disorder is as delicate and unique as, *"The snow flakes that fall from the heavens, out of all that have fallen, there mysterious individualism still can not be explained"*...LD-Disorders also have a cunning ability to become an imbedded negative thought that changes our children's feelings about themselves as they painfully slip between the cracks of their scholastics days. *"Unless their lucky enough to have someone like you who's looking out for them"*...Your awareness, the unsettled heartstrings you carry, the familiarities of a path once traveled and your ever present voice. The voice that will ultimately become that child's life jacket. *"And that my friend is what brings you here today,"*...as you search for that some type of unknown, possibly some written words of validation to help you, them or that someone you know. There will be a few among all the small scholastics faces and the emotional turmoil that comes with *LD,* whom will find a delicate beam of light and that light will wash over them, forming waves of colors slowly replacing their darkness within them. Its clarity will radiate while strengthening their courage and self-esteem inside of them and in you, reveling an uncharted path that you will take together; hands-in-hand and one foot in front of the other, one step forward your child will take and you as their voice, beside them. Soon the both of you are on your way, discovering, conquering and sharing what may come. While doing so, you will have wrapped your arms around your child securing their welfare, as you both begin a journey that will span their scholastic years, until one day they become their own voice and chart their own path for the next to come. And somewhere along the way, with your guidance and patience's they might just find a spectacular pot of shiny-self, hidden away, beneath all of his or her learning disorders, self-rubble and debris.

This book your about to read for yourself or to that someone you know, is not about the scientific or medical explanation of Learning Differences / Disabilities nor is it about those professionals whom debit over its existence / therapy and its not about House Bill 157 or OSER ACT of 1973.

"There's a variety of that type of reading out there already."

This book is about; *LDs,* powerful tidal wave of emotions that comes with everyday obstacles after milestone days are long gone. The overwhelming undercurrents that hides beneath the invisible tears of failure that fall because, *"He or She are trying their best, but their mind, senses and body mechanics are not functioning together like a team, ever so getting in their way of learning how to write, spell, read and playing"* …The layers of innocent scars, brought on by unsuccessful attempts to do better, over what can not be seen or wished way. The feeling of being inadequate starts to build and their foundation beings to crack unable to hold their form, slowly chipping away at a new and unstable self. Unfortunately accumulating patterns of disappointments with every year, with every grade and try as they may, catching up becomes less and less reachable for them. Disappearing and fading away into themselves hoping to keep from feeling disappointment. *LD* has all the capability to expose overwhelming negative emotions, as *it* leaves behind rippling damages, effortlessly takes hold of their spirit convincing them of want they are not and what they can't achieve. *"That of which I speak of, can not be felt by those who haven't walked in our children's shoes,"* Then as though that wasn't enough for our children to deal with. There might come a time when they may over hear the sound of crushing words from those they look up to. As those adults attempt to convince and explain to us, their parents, *"He or She just needs to apply themselves more,"* with their words of misdirected helpfulness, ill-compassion and misinformed knowledge, as they safely set with out hesitation behind the their desk rubbing away the natural shine from an apple, oblivious to their words and how truly deep *LD* cuts away at their student's soul and our children inner image of themselves. *"The struggling attempts of getting no where fast, circling within a whirlpool of self-blame, self-disappointments and helplessness"*

Then just when it seems the turmoil will never break, some how it does and subsequently by chance or other, a child may have a surprising advocate encounter with people along their career path as a student, who quietly and creatively assist them to be the best that they can be, ever so watchful of those others around them. *"They are the true essences of the word Teacher; they who can adapt their skills and experience, by applying and teaching every one of their students as an individual but also as a collective group. Miraculous combining and helping them make sense of their topsy-tury worlds altogether, along with their students input and talents, magically empowering them with self-worth and knowledge....To have LD is also to be Extraordinarily-Different and from that with encouragement can emerge visionaries, the out of the box thinkers, which may lead to; Authors, Writers, Out of sync Geniuses, Teachers, Inventors, Artiest, Entertainers, Musicians, Athletes,* Designers, Scientists, and the list goes on and on," …

This book is about my son's first nine years with his *inherited-genetic-kink,* a part of my self, I unwillingly passed on to him. The subtle differences at first, the ones we choose to ignore due to our own; Fear, Denial, Ignorance or maybe simply because we managed to live through our childhood with *it, "Subconsciously detached with it's over all affect and consequences,"*...Then later the more obvious out of sync devolvement skills that may appear and persisted long after early childhood milestone moments have pasted. The awkward body mechanics lacking in coordination and organizations unseen and left behind. Those skills that should have been mastered long ago but for what ever reason weren't. Your lives move on and it's the first day of school, time to learn their ABC's and 123's. But no one could have prepared your child and you for the long road ahead and the confusing encounters.

"You might just be, LD if singing the Alphabet song, is the only way, you can remember, your ABCs,"...School days, with its population, pace and demands begins to exposes numerous facets of this disorder, encounters that have even puzzled experts. When *LD* beginnings to appear, *it* will emotionally drain you and make you question your parental care and your child, if your not vigilant. *"Living with LD, is forever, for the moment you take in your first breath until you take your last, it doesn't go away, We just learn how "to-go-with-it" as we get older by using; Dictionaries, Calculators, Our wits, people around us, "I forgot my glasses will you read this for me", Friends, Technology etc...We also learn as we get older, what works for one person may not work for another, There's not a Guide book or a Manuel, that can prepare anyone for the unraveling and emotional clashes that will come, You either learn how to Modify, Accommodate and Adapted to stay afloat or drown"* ...

Our journey and experiences, with that part of ourselves which is very much real but oh-so extremely; Incompliant, Complicated, Misdiagnosed, Misunderstood, Unbelievable and often overlooked. It's difficult to explain Learning Differences / Disability and all that comes with it, to those individuals whom haven't inherited its genetic-kinks, with all its scholastics impairments, possible physical out of sync's, and emotional impacts. The perplexity doesn't stop there, because somewhere along the way you might stubble across that unexpected sliver lining that also accompanies *LD*, the gifts and talents that usually don't appear until fundamental elementary days are gone. *"LD is the ultimate oxymoron,"*... So how do we teach children to cope with what is beyond their understanding at such an early age. They who are limited in the ability to express with words and not their emotions how

11

and why they can't achieve what other children / peers their age can.

"Acceptance, Confidence and Self-Worth are feeling about ourselves that can not be taught or learned, it manifests its-self from deep within us,"… We acquire the feel-good about self response from our peers, our surroundings and the reactions of our actions. Those important sparks that light us up from inside that praises us for a job will done. That self-good-feeling spark, gives us the courage and the drive to reach out and challenge our abilities further, to conquer and achieve new goals so we can relive that sensation once again. But for most students with *LD*, positive feed-back doesn't ignited sparks of confidences. Instead the opposite occurs, the unsuccessful attempts of not achieving a goal, prevents them from trying again. Unfortunately that positive-self reinforcement responds is not an emotion many of our children with *LD* experience until much later in life. *"It's a tragedy when you're a child, to never feel good about who you are because of an unseen and unidentified disorder, you were born with. To truly expose LD in its complete grandeur, and put an end to the hurtful imprints it leaves upon them, We who have history with hurtful torturing school days of long ago once filled with self blame wishing to be someone else or somewhere else, can make a difference by voicing and sharing, "A task, our-inner-child, is unwilling to relive or remember"* …

Until one day we let our guard down and through the long thick lashes unable to hold the tears back any longer. You watch as his slouchy small frame approaches. "There was something seriously wrong," bewildered by his unrecognizable stature, the alarms in my head started to go off and my parental imagination could only think the worst. As his quivering lips and wounded voice attempted to speak, but didn't. Bracing myself, "I asked him what was wrong," He began by saying, "I have a secrete to tell you." Then he continued, by asking for my forgiveness for something he didn't mean to do and didn't understand why or how it happened. Looking down at him you feel your knees weaken as you try to hold back your anxiety, briefly being lost for words as your mind races. Then he hands you a work sheet, he had been hiding behind his back. "Only for a few seconds, a feeling of relief comes over you as the pounding in your chest slows down," Then you focus on that white work sheet, as you compose yourself, not expecting what you were about to see in plain sight. There it was right in front of you once again, your heart starts to race and your throat tights. But this time, it's your son's name on that paper with bold red checks marked all over it and that capital red letter grade, shouting its negative-scolding's that brings it all back.

"It was in that moment of our vulnerability," You recognize your own memories being played back, reel by reel in your beautiful little brown eyes looking up at you for love, guidance and forgiveness. There I saw, a flash back of my own soul crushing and dreadful school days of long ago forgotten and locked away so many years before him. I thought it was all behind me, the sweaty hands, my stomach sinking down to my toes, the headaches, the stomachaches, always wishing to be invisible. Longing to be someone else and faraway, trying desperately not to bring attention to myself as, *Mrs. X, hovered ever so smoothly among us, like a predator in open water waiting for just the right moment to lash out and devour the weakest who dared set in her classroom, while sweating* blood bullets, I would set as still as possible praying not to be seen," Humiliation and Embracement lived within me keeping my dumbness company, unable to learn all because of me, wishing desperately not to be exposed in front of the world to see and the eyes that lived among me, judging every word and action that came from me. I became an expert on bathroom breaks and timing, escaping though the door right before it was my turn to participate. I shamefully gave up to the guilt and the pressures of being me, no more would I prepare by counting the paragraphs then rehearing the words to myself before called upon. No more, would I raise my hand with the correct answer, only to be scolded and laughed at because the words would come out wrong. The inability to show my work was also against me because even when it was right, it was wrong. I failed at studying too, it just wouldn't stay in my head, long enough to past any test or assignment, numbers and letters danced and played, losing me along the way. I escaped by painfully becoming invisible. I didn't want anyone to see, how dumbness lived in side of me. There in my bedroom on that autumn day, I dropped to my knees, wrapped my arms around my son and felt a waterfall of tears falling inside me for him and what was sure to come. He held tightly to my neck as he whispered in my ear, "Mom, I just can't read, please don't be mad at me, I try, but I can't," he said as his cry fell down on my shoulder and into my heart, melting away the cemented secrete and fears. *"Students with LD can distinguish that something is wrong, even when they don't know what it is"*...I held him even tighter and said, "I believe you my son, and it's going to be okay." Then just like that, without hesitation, I decided, *"Not my Child"*

"This is our story; we truly hope it inspires you to share your experiences while being your child's voice,"

I remember clearly that March spring day, it was the first Saturday after my daughters eighteenth birthday, which was February 28 during that same week day, so we had decided to delay her celebration until that weekend. It was a perfect day for a party, the spring weather was cooperating and all was right in our world. By the time the drinks had been iced and the barbeque pit was ready, it was about three o'clock in the afternoon. We had been anticipating my son's arrival for two and a half weeks to no avail. My daughter did all that should could to encourage her little brother's appearance before her birthday celebration. We walked; climbed stairs and she even went as far as driving me over rough country terrain in her sporty short bed pickup truck, all the while reminding me not to give birth to her baby brother during her party. Will, that's exactly what happened, as the party started, her father and herself were driving me to the hospital the same one she had been born in a little over eighteen years ago. We walked through the double emergence doors at three-thirty in the afternoon, expecting to be sent back home after a few hours but this third time around would bring our addition. At six-thirty, after a slight hesitation due to umbilical intanglment he was born that same day. I had given birth for the second time of my life at the age of thirty-seven; with my husband and our daughter at my side we welcomed our new little member to our family. By then we had forgotten all about the party, and suddenly three days later we were being wheeled out though the front doors and with a good bye and a smile we were on our way home. It didn't take long before we settled into our new routine, days became months and soon it was time for Baby Well Check appointments and Immunizations. What a blessing, there hadn't been any serous injuries or illness before or after his birth. My son hadn't even experience any of those childhood ones either; he was always the perfect picture of health. Milestones days started rolling by; days of teething and replacing baby clothes became part of the norm. Soon he was discovery himself, toes, fingers and ears. He especially liked his ears always tugging and touching them. Then one day by accident, we noticed how he would instinctively cover his ears at any loud noise inside our home and when we were out and about too. "All of my healthy pregnancy care, reading to him aloud and listing to music while we were one, might have encouraged his cleverness, just like all the books had read," Then come the first subtle hints of his uniqueness. *"Crawling is a gross motor skill that requires manipulation of aims and legs oppositely moving together in a sequence,"*... A coordination and development skill my son didn't learn, instead he learned how to scoot on his bottom and on his back or he would roll to where he wanted to go. Soon he was standing then walking, he had skipped the traditional crawl stage, and he had bypassed the crawl before you walk, "How smart was he." Throughout his first years other coordination skill appeared slightly off and unbalanced but ,"He also was over alert and bright for his age," and according to books, all children learn at a different pace and no one seemed to be concerned but me, including his Pediatricians. Their logic and responds was always the same; Boys tend to be a little lazy, give him time, Its been eighteen years since there's been a toddler in the house, its bound to be different and He's your first boy its going to be different and don't worry, he's healthy so relax. Their words didn't feel right to me, but it had been along time and maybe, I was just being overly sensitive. I was nursing him so maybe that bond between a mother and her child, had brought out my apprehension feelings too, I convinced myself. Learning to talk was a challenge for him too, but at the time, it sounded like cutie baby talk, but in reality he wasn't encoding and decoding sound of letters correctly. *"Processing each sound of a letter to its word is the key to copying and learning to speak"*...Instead he would miss sounds or mistaking letter and there sounds for example; B for V as in the word *vanilla* he would pronounce as *banilla* also T for N and T for C, "Pronunciations of words was just another adorable part of being himself, so we believed at the time" He was very good at memory games and repeating sequences, so for every slight concern, there was an advice action or responds on his part to eliminate my concern. Time went on and enrollment for Pre-K was upon us. He liked socialize and making friends. His natural intelligences, large vocabulary and out going personality was quickly notice by his teacher and her aid. There were some concerns with his mispronunciations of sounds, letter and number confusion but they were confident he would catch up, because of how bright he was. Pre-K ended with great expectations and a kit flying party. By the middle of Kindergarten, his block writing was less then others and his motor/fine gross skills too. He was still confusing letters and numbers, for example; F-T, W-V-M-N, D-C-O, P-B, c-o b-d, 1-I-L, y-v, q-p, 2-5, h-u-n and 8-S also h-4 (the traditional number four). Coloring within the lines was still difficult to do along with cutting, tracing shapes plus he couldn't rhyme. *"Phonological issues can at times be dedicated by the inability to Rhyme"*...By the end of that school year his coordination skills had not improved; bouncing a ball, walking a line foot to toe, jumping jacks, his balance and control of body movements were still awkward. His hesitation to play on the playground equipment wasn't surprising to me, because he had never been a tuff and tumble kind of boy, *"He did try and in doing so missed a step and sprained is right ankle and that was that"*... As the end of the year approached one of his teachers came forward one day and stated, *"He's to smart not to be smart,"*...a phrase, I had never heard before. Then she told me the story about a family member who too was, "To smart not to be smart too" the challenges and stress all her family shared, due to the unique one among them. Her words were genuine and kind as she stressed the importance of staying on top of his impairments, "If that's what it was" She praised his natural intelligence as many had done in the passed and soon the year was over. Summer came and we practiced with flash cards, reading, writing and coloring. I didn't recognize any visible issues or problems as we practiced thought out the days, at a pace comfortable for him and without any distractions. We moved him to a new campus due to possible building and health issues at the previous one. Through out the weeks, he was excited about going to a new school and making new friends. My son's personality has always been enthusiastic, respectful and charming. His good behavior and vocabulary skills always made him seem older then what he was too, he also displayed signs of incredible memorization too. First grade year started but by the third month he had become the opposite of himself. He was unhappy and he didn't want to go to school anymore. Losing interested in everything he enjoyed plus the thought of going to school made him cry. Coincidently that was also about the time their teacher started to wean them off their kindergarten mode. Plus spelling words became four, five, and six letters and more complex from what he was use to, *" No longer could he spell by memorizing nor could he read by prediction an act many LD's do"* the speed in which lessons were being taught had increased and when time was up, it was on to the next one. During the parent conference, the explanations was, "The adjustment from K to First is big and it can take time for some children to adjust" the impression was he had plenty of time to improve his declining grades.

It had been a little over three months, since we had talked through the doors of his new school. By all indications he was ready to take on first grade, to make new friends and to learn. But slowly his mood had changed. He didn't want to go school and didn't want to practice at home anymore either. He had become an unhappy child who wasn't full of eagerness and curiosity what had happened to my boy. "Nothing could have prepared me for the emotional and mind blowing epiphany, that was about to happened," in the house with the green door where we lived. *"It had skipped my first child, like their father, a true teachers dream pupil straight A's from the beginning, A Rae of light that came from me, but no out-of-the box characteristics like her little brother, who was solid as a Roc, so surly it had skipped him too, that part of myself, I refused to share with either one of them, I prayed and wished, they would have more of their father in them then me"* ... There we were back in my bedroom arms wrapped around each other on that Autumn day, "Two individuals thrown together by chance and entangled by our Genetic-Straps.".. That next morning, I walked through the campus door unaware of the battle in front us. I wasn't sure how to go about finding out, what was going on or who to ask for assistance for his benefit, but that wasn't going to stop me. It all began with meetings after meetings with several administrators. Then finally after my continual insisting, it was agreed. He would be given a non official assessment test by the one of their people; it would determine where he racked among students his age and grade level. According to the understanding of it, the test would also give us a clue to any hidden issues that could be contributing to his failing grades. Soon after we were all in agreement and he was tested. Finally the phone call came that we had been waiting for. A follow up meeting was schedule to discuss the results of the assessment. I approached the meeting confident, "Surly It had skipped my son, just like It had skipped my daughter so many years ago," even though my instintics were screaming, "He has It and You gave It to him," But until a professional confirmed my suspicions, It didn't exist. I was invited in and asked to set down then she began. Page by page she reviewd and recalled my son's answeres. The eveluation had determined where my son's was, compared to other school children his age. The counslor was delighted on how high he had scored on; intelligence, vocabulary, comprehension and his ability to carry a conversation was impressive; she also made a point of discussing his attention to detail. He had been the only student, since she could remember, who had asked, "Why she had a fishless fish bowl in her room," an observation no one had bothered to ask about before. His scores were low in writing, reading and spelling, though same of those low scores fluctuate depending on the word or words, "I believe, she was as confussed as I was, his inconsistencies just didn't add up" She explained how some children need a little more time to get the process of reading, writing and spelling down and because my son scored high in the other areas. She suggested he might just need some more time for all of it to click together and maybe he just needed sometime to mature too. For the time being, patiences and practicing was the recommendation, "At the time, it didn't sound or feel right," but my wishful thinking didn't want him to have any problems, so I agreed. Time passed and though work, I started to network with individuals in the educational realm asking their opinion and thoughts in the matter. Meanwhile my son's grades and temperament was spiraling down without improvement. School days were filled with unhappyness and tears, gone was that cheerful boy eager to learn. Then one day at work someone told me about a hospital known worldwide for its dedication to children impairments. The waiting list is long they told me, but onces your in, they would officially test, diagnose and sign on the dotted line on their patience's behalf. I contacted them, and a few weeks later a large 8x10 manila envelope arrived in the mail. *"That phone call, would become the most significant and important step toward bring clarity and help to my son"*...The identification of his *LD* would ultimately bring me face to face with what seemed like an unexpected up hill battle.

"The beginnings of my son's academic future came with that one phone call,"...I continued meeting with my son's administrators. But to no avail, their answer was always the same, "He just needs time to mature and he's sure to catch up" I could see my son was sinking at a alarming rate and for as much as I tried, I couldn't keep him afloat for very long with out him breaking loose and plummeting down again. *"We parents know our children better then anyone so don't ever allow anyone to tell you otherwise"*...

Time slowly passed, and my child's campus became very familiar with my voice and face, as I constantly reminded them of my concerns. "Then came a break in our rolling storm clouds," The much awaited phone call, an appointment had been schedule just for him. A two day, eight hour evaluation by their facility's top children specialist was reserved just for him. *"Finally some peace of mind for my bright son, and the truth, I didn't want to face"*...During this time, I had been explaining to my son and reassuring him the testing would not be, a paper grade type of test, he would be allowed plenty of time to answer. Then to ease his anxiety, I briefly described what type of doctors would be evaluating him and how important it was for us to know how his mind and body worked together. There would be no injection or medicine to take either. He had already been seen by two other doctors who didn't give him any injections or medication; the eye and the hearing specialist, so he understood. I did all in my power to make sure he was comfortable with what was about to happen.

The third appointment was made, this four hour session was to discuss his test results, diagnoses, recommendations and any questions parents may have. As we waited to be called back my son played with some interactive toys, carefree and happy. And all I could do was pray, "Please let *it* have skipped him, Please don't let him be like me, Please don't let him have *it*,"…We were greeted and called back by Ms. PH.D, first without my son, then later he would be asked to join us. First she wanted us to know that out of a group of two-hundred school age students K-12th our son scored in the top eighteen for higher intelligences then she said, Your son perceives information in 3'D and also " When most people see a glass half full or half empty," your son looks at that same glass and sees very possible questions that could be asked of it, for example; is the liquid water or clear carbonated soda, and if its soda which one, who might have poured it and how long ago, had anyone drank from it and was the amount in the glass the bottom half or was it poured half way on purpose, who dose it belong to etc...Then she congratulated us for our brilliant boy and the pleasure it had been to have visited with him. She gave us his file and then she began explaining each page, stopping along the way to answer any questions. Then came their professional diagnoses "The tears came and washed out every bit of that rose color haze, from my brown eyes as every drop fell," when I heard her say, my son was *Dyslexic* with a Handwriting problem, the early signs of *Dysgraphia* but because of his age only time would tell if there was other disorders, I wept for him, for the long road ahead and the traveled road, but especially out of guilt for giving it to him"...Ms. PH.D was kind to share her tissues, tears and compationate words before inviting my son back to join the conversation. She briefly recounted the test and what was concluded from it. Then when she explained, how smart he was, and how all that testing proofed, he had been trying his very best at school. My son enthusiastically smiled and hollered, *"Yes! I knew it mom!" "I knew something was wrong and I knew! I was trying my best!"* At that moment his excitement changed my tears into joy for him. In that conference room, history was being made, by changing the future for a little boy in first grade. *"At his young age, he understood he was not dumb, he knew he had told the truth about trying his best* and *he heard and learned how smart he really was,"*...On the drive home, I shared in more detail how difficult school had been for me and how a part of learning also depends on our brain, eyes, and hands all working together like a team and without one of those players the team is uncompleted, trying my best not to overwhelm him. We left that afternoon, with copies of the summary on my son and recommendations for his school campus, plus the knowledge of how he learns by visual, auditory and memorization. *"Each LD child is as different as they are a like, and that likeness is what brings us together"*...Armed with all this valuable information and medical/scientific proof from educated professionals in the field of *Neurobological Disorders* from a will known and respected children's facility. We were ready for the next step. It was nearly spring break by the time we had all of my son's testing and diagnoses in order, his first grade year was almost gone by then. He had spent from October on struggling with assignments and himself. No longer could he memorize his spelling words due to there complexity. The written and spoken language we speak and read is much more complicated then what it seems, *"It's not just about Phonics, we just think it is"*...

The only consultation at the time was his handwriting was about in the same range of some of the other students, so at the time there wasn't much focused on it yet. By the time the campus planned a meeting to discuss my son's academic impairments and how they were going to address those issues and to ensure his success as their student. It was the week after spring break, and after all, my son had been through, I was ready for their commitment. The campus committee wouldn't agree to any of the recommendations on his summary, reasoning being it was too soon to tell if his issues wouldn't catch up with his intelligence, considering it to early would due more damage then good. The responds didn't make sense to me, "Better sooner then later" One positive action and improvement that came from that meeting, was removing my son from one particular classroom and environment. The second was forgetting my parental manners and transforming into, *"A Loin"* I drove to the building that houses the people whose responsibility and job is to assure an equal education opportunity for each and every student in our public schools. I waited somewhere between thirty-five and forty minutes before being seen. I greeted the person by shaking hands and by doing so noticed a proudly displayed collage ring still being worn. I introduced myself as the parent of, and then commenced sharing my son's situation and concerns. It was evident, I hadn't capture the undivided attention my son deserved, feeling at the brink of being invisible, *"The Loin roared,"* By asking, "If there was any personal knowledge and familiarity with *LD*," Then I decided to shared one of my favorite analogies on the emotional impact of having *LD* and this is what I said, *"Imagine,* its time for your yearly physical and even though it's the same old doctor from years ago, you still can't help but feel embarrassed as you stand, clinching on to the waist band of your dry clean trouser trying to prepare yourself for the humiliating spread-eagle possession, suddenly a knock comes to the door and in comes that blue eyed blonde headed girl that went to school with your daughter not so long ago and she's your doctor's assistant," and there it was, the attention my son deserved. By the end of that conversation, and the next academic day my son had been granted accommodations and modifications, also know as a 504 plan. *"It shouldn't take analogies of any kind to remind those or enlighten them, of the extreme humiliation, embarrassment and physiological impact our LD children / student endure in our public schools and their academic years,"* It was near the end of first grade by now. My son was slowly becoming happy and eager to get to school again, through networking, becoming informed and keeping as close as possibly to his *LD* summary he was on his was back. For his benefit he needed to attend a campus where the *LD* Therapist was in house, which would give him four days a week of *LD*-Therapy, not one hour twice a week if the travling therapist made it on time. Therefore a transfer and a move was the next step. It was time for second grade all the preplanning had been made. A new school, *LD* Therapist in house, four days a week of therapy, plus many faces among those hallways with the ability, experience, compassion and maybe a few with personal knowledge on how to accommodate many type of students and their learning needs, including *LD* too. Once again my son was eager to learn, make new friends and to go school. I also invested some appropriate tools for his challages; triangle shape pencils, colors, learning through Listening with audio book programs available for those persons and students with learning difference / disability plus feeding his mind and senses too. When second grade ended, he had been prasied by many, his paper grades had improved, and there had been a slight mention of his natural intelligences overriding his disorder, *"It's only an allusion, LD just doesn't stop and go way"*...I listened to the suggestion but did not comment to any such ideal, it was too soon to tell. *"As certain as the tide changes, so does the ups and downs of LD"*...By third grade year, my confidence in being my son voice had strengthened and my knowleged in *Dyslexia, Dyscalculia, Dysgraphia* and *Dyspraxia* had grown too. I became better familiar with the policies and the names of the people who represents our students with *LD,* The Dyslexia Handbook, Net-Working with other Parents, becoming aware of our states Education Agency, State and Federal Contacts and Our Regional Educational Services too. I had also managed to keep an intense collation of my son's school work through out each years, notes from meetings, e-mails, physician examination, copies of all important papers that dismissed ADHD / ADD and visual and audio inadequacies and finally keeping curtain with all paper trail that would validate my son's *LD, "Proving what isn't LD is just as important as proving it is LD and make no mistake of it, no one will be or can be your Childs voice but you"*...Third grade year, that's right about the time our children start letting go of our hand as they walk beside us. Never more will they be that young age again, where they relay on you alone for all their needs. Gone are the days of tying shoes laces, rights from lefts and awkward motor skills. For many of our children at this grade level, they start recognizing themselves as their own individual and not just a part of the group. They begin responding to the sparks from a job well done. The introduction to acquiring their self-worth and value, as they achieve and accumulate that positive feeling, with every successful task asked of them or that of which they ask of themselves.

"My son's LD, is not my LD and my LD, is not your LD and that's what sets us apart but LD is what Brings us Together as One"...It was during third grade year my son discovered his *LD*-differences there among his peers and among himself then decided he didn't want it anymore. He was fortunate to have an educator who understood his unique dilemma through out the long year. He became fatigued easily in the classroom, complaining about everything and everyone being too loud, unwilling to participate and not wanting to be excused for *LD*-Therapy. No longer where there conversations about how will he was doing, Now the conversations were geared toward, how can we keep his walls from going up and shutting everyone out. There was countless day of my son not feeling good a combination of; headaches, stomachaches, diarrhea, not eating or over eating, unable to sleep and when he did, only to be awaken by nightmares. He was experiencing real symptom of being sick without a medical diagnose of any illness. *"The stress our children / students with LD feel is real and it shows itself in many* forms"... Meanwhile, he was still having trouble with fine and gross motor skills too, a milestone many children conquer before second grade. Holding a pencil, fork, toothbrush, hair comb and any small object was difficult for him to manipulate with his hands and fingers. Buttons, zippers and lacing was also a huge challenge for his mind, eyes, and fingers. *"It all has to work together in*

order to accomplish a simple task"…Then came a break in the clouds again, rummaging though books at the half price store. I found some clarity, the next day, setting in at his gym period; there it was loud and clear in plain sight. Compared to other children his age my son's coordination had not grown with him. He was clumsy out of sync, he's gross motor skills were lacking in proficiency as will as his fine motor skills too, "Know I understood why he didn't like going to P.E. class. I also noticed other anxieties with the stairs and the tile floor. I asked him about it and this is what he said, *"Mom, everything is always moving and it confuses me, so I move slow, because I don't want to fall." "Perception and Multi Sensory Disorders / Impairments perhaps Hyper or Hypo, can and may accompany the LD child"*…The trick is, recognizing it as just that and getting your child approved yet again. The stressful waters of that year didn't quite down until the end. Between preparation for the end of the year testing and a fractured right ankle sustained somewhere between school hours and pick-up time, you can bet, *"His Lion came foreword once again,"*… *Blessed are our children who indure eight hours a day, five days a week and ten months out of a year, in an enviroment that may or may not openly understand them and seems to be always looking for a reason not to accommodate them for their unseen disability and disorders, they are the unseen heroes that quietly walk within their educational hallways*… *"To subjected an LD child to conventional summer school, without supervision by an LD-Therapist, is to subjected a student to torture"*…Summer break and once again practicing was on the agenda but also taking him back to basics as some books, parents and *LD*-Therapist recommended through my ever so present networking chain. Back to the Milestones, he had missed so many years ago. Back to relearning fine and motor skills from holding a small object in his hands to crawling across the floor. Also staying in practicing with what came natural to him; memorization, facts, details, creativity, imagination and his large word vocabulary and conversational skills. By the time jackets were being worn, my fourth grader was wearing laces shoes and zip up jeans. The hallway tiles and stairs didn't seem such an enormous obstacle anymore. Then came more testing per my request; sensory processing and occupational therapy for his handwriting expression. A few more classroom accommodations were added too; Gold Overlay for reading, Book Marks, Letter Spacer and always volunteer reading aloud and no bold red pin markings. *"The Red markings on school-work sheets is a clear visual indication of Failure that Screams out to those impressible little eyes and There's not a child that should ever feel that way about themselves, LD or not LD"*...It hasn't been easy for my son, with his extraordinary marvelous mind that doesn't match the rest of him, "Having a high I.Q. has opened him up to his own contradictions". My words at times didn't console his frustrations with himself and especially with his fingers. *"Where was the gifts many LD specialist and books talk about, he needed a self made boost, LD plus A High I.Q. Is a difficult combination to live with, your quickly accused as not doing your best"* ...

Determined to help him with his fine motor skills, the most unexpected event happened. He found his gift, "The gift that comes with LD"... without looking for it. It was in a small nine dollar box of multicolor bricks. At first he refused to even try to stack the small pieces together because his fingers would cooperate and picture reading the instructions was working either. Then one day he said, "I'm just going to look at the picture on the box and build it," and soon the bricks came together picture perfect. The triumph he felt, catapulted him to want to try more sets and video games too. A spark of positive self worth had started to grow inside him again. I could see a glow of success beaming from his beautiful brown eyes for finishing a task will done. A part of himself, he alone can only encourage, I hadn't been able to reach in a long time. By the end of year one of son's biggest accomplishment happened because of him and this is what he said, "Mom, today at school we had a substitute, and she asked me to read aloud, I answered her by saying, "I'm Dyslexic and I have trouble with reading, I also have a 504 so would you please ask someone else to read," and then she smiled at me and did just that," It made me feel good, that she believed me and that nobody laughed." On the drive home from school that day my son made this observation about us *LD's. "We LD's (Dyslexics) are like snowflakes Mom, We are as different as we are alike and we have such a long way to travel and none of us take the same highway getting there"*... I looked over at my son and there in his brown eyes were the first signs of accepting along road ahead of him. Fifth grade year is soon to start, once again he's been practicing on school skills throughout the break along with trying to conquer balancing on his bike plus he's up to six-hundred plus pieces of tiny confident building bricks. This is his last year in elementary, where the foudation of all students' scholastic career is imprinted within themselves and their self value and worth becomes an important part of their being. I don't know what this year will bring for him. I just know, "I'll walk beside him every step of the way being his Voice and Lion when need be. This isn't the end of a mother's story or her son's journey with his Learning Differences / Disabilities and all different facets that comes with it. It's just a pause on the LD highway, until the light changes and we're off again…..To be continued.

" I believe, until the World of Education truly and openly shows there acceptance of *LD* by adding *LD*-Training for all future and present teachers also making *LD* -Training a collage requirement / credit before becoming an Educator for K-12th, Placing an *LD*-Therapist in each public school campus, eliminating the traveling *LD*-Therapist and the Umbrella Clause too, allowing *LD* support groups for students and parents within the districts and the acceptances of early *LD* testing and finally adding a *"Gifted-Class"* for the Unconventional Scholastic students who carry their strengths in a Sliver Lining with in them. Until then there will continue to be students / children that fall inbetween the cracks forgotten and unseen and they will be left behind, accompanied only by their *LD*-Shadow….

…"How do they deprogram learning habits and skills from an impressionable establish student, then re-teach them how to learn according to their individual disorder, then convince them they are not dumb,"…The Sooner the Better

...Person to Person...

- *You know your child better then anyone.*

- *You are your child's only voice; he or she will not be accommodated for their LD without you.*

- *Allow yourself to be accepting of that genetic-kink within the family.*

- *Forgive yourself.*

- *LD Therapy classes, the sooner the better, who can not totally erase the inner child's negative perception about themselves and habits already learned.*

- *Get informed, search for material to help you, help your child.*

- *Eliminate the obvious possibilities; eye sight, hearing, and behavioral. (ADD and ADHAD)*

- *Search for those facitly and people that will evaluate your child.*

- *Inform your child, so one day they can be their own voice.*

- *Get to know your child's district and the people within it who represent are students with Learning Differences / Disabilities and its Disorders.*

- *Sometimes the people within your child's scholastic years may be able or unable to do what we parents insist.*

- *Sometimes the people in your child's scholastic years may look at their career as just a job.*

- *Sometimes the people in your child's scholastic years may do more for them then their own parents.*

- *Sometimes the people in your child's scholastic years will collaborate and work to provide the best possible education for their LD student.*

- *Search for help from your states, county and region, LD is recognized as a Disability "OSER of 1973 and House Bill of 157".*

- *Keep a paper-trail file, on your child.*

- *Share with others.*

- *Remember during the scholastic years while your discovering the D's in LD it will be exhausting, "Like walking though water with jeans on"*

- *Find that Sliver Lining, within your child.*

- *Never give up because without you, your child has on one.*

The intent within the pages of this book is only to
share our experience and to confirm you are not alone
on your journey for clarity on the LD Highway….

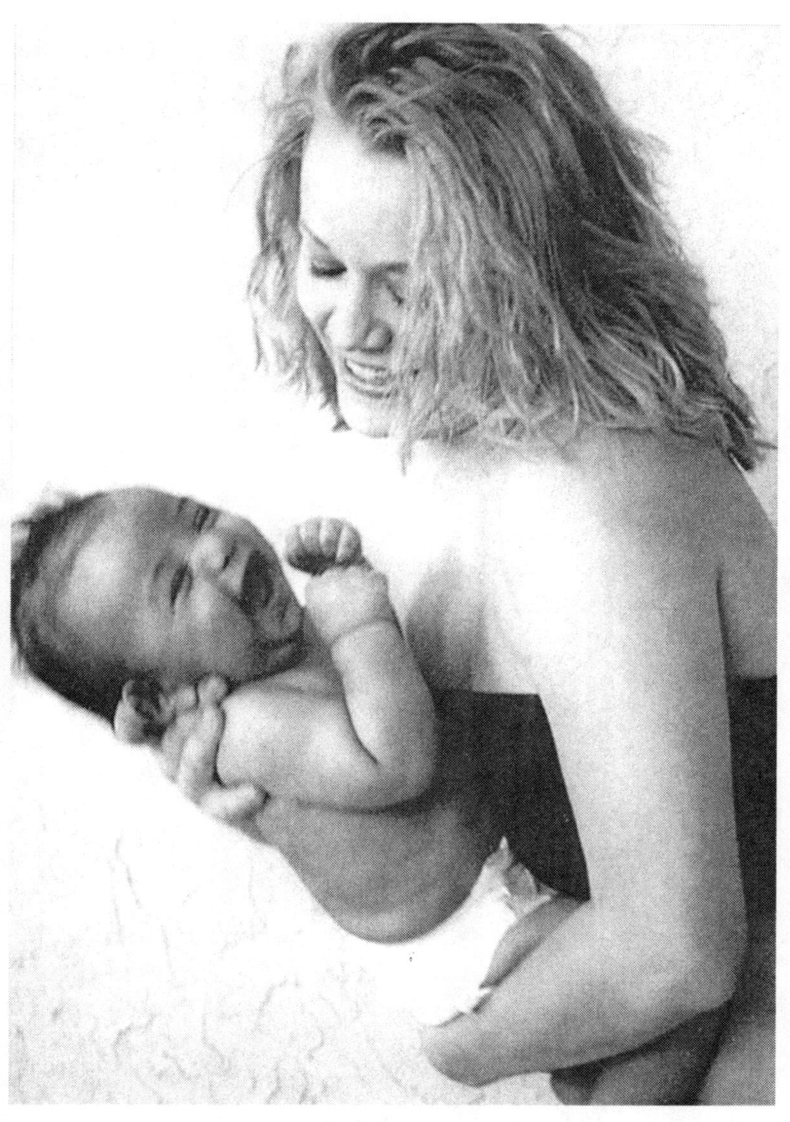

The Rae of light that illuminated my darkness and my little
Roc who broke down my fears.
"Son el ritmo di mi Corazon"

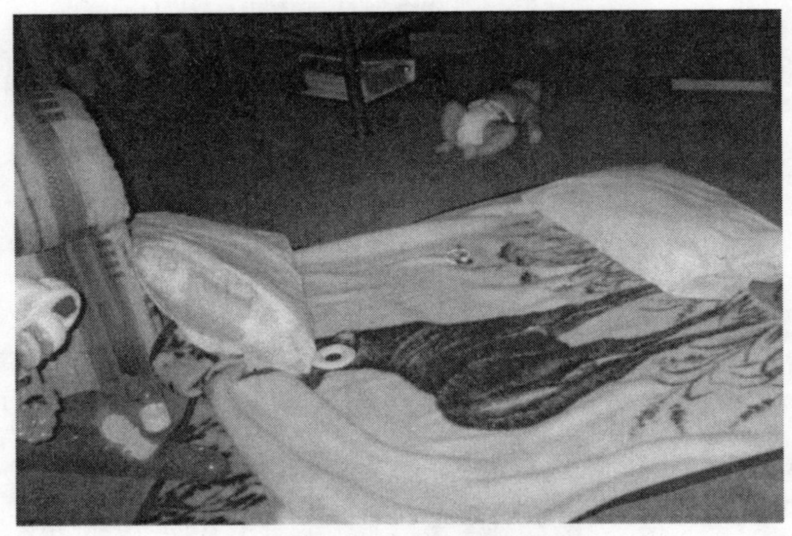

"Back scooting"

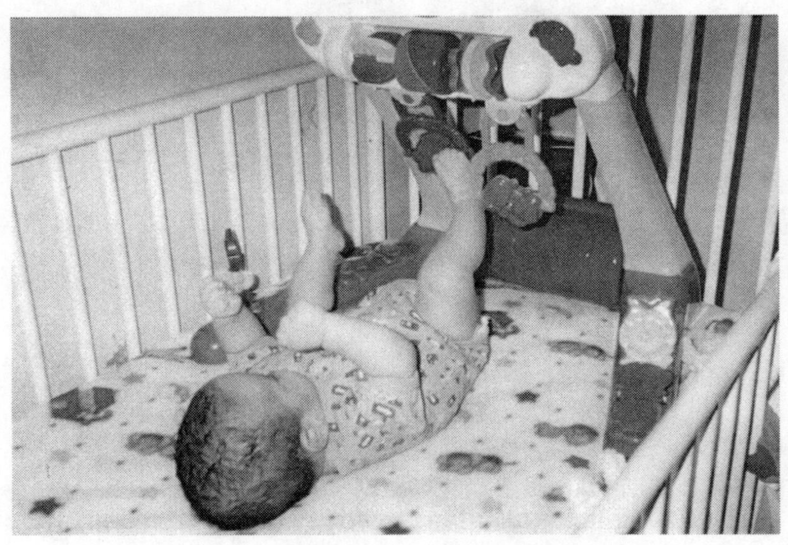

"How smart was he"

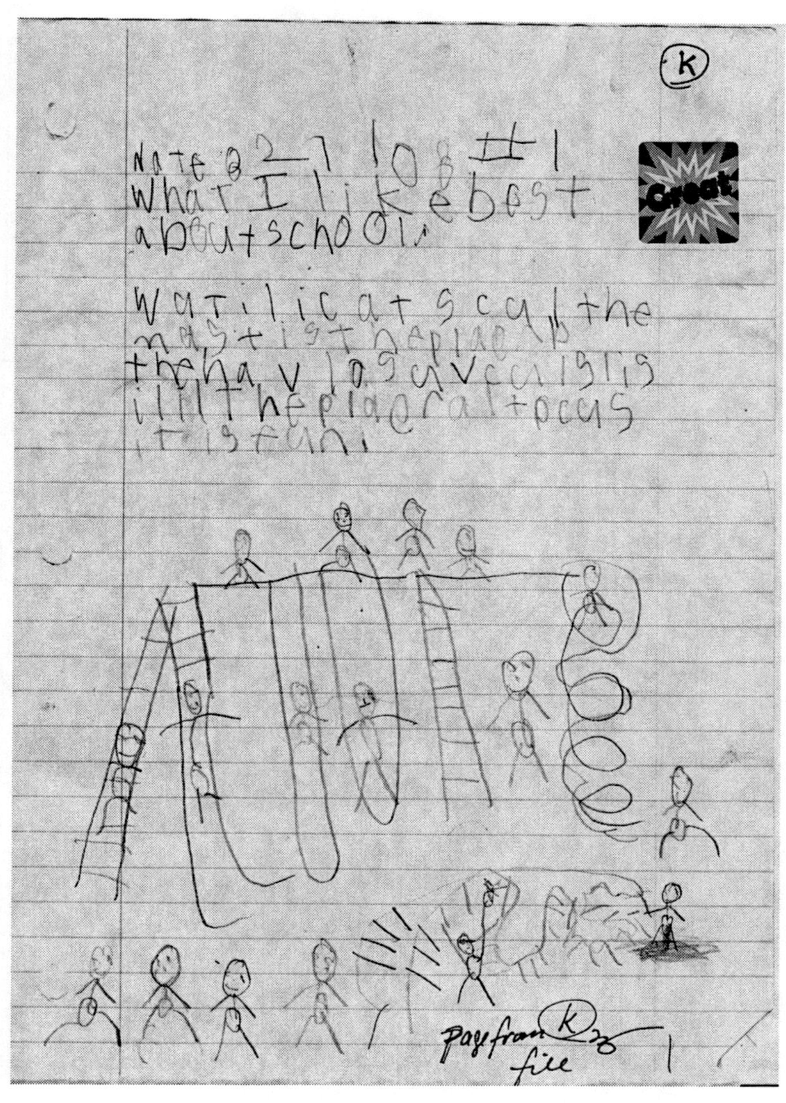

First grade was a tough-tough year,
we decided not to share work pages.

Nate 1st hw (2nd)

100

Nate,
You worked
very hard! Thank
you for working
so hard!

3. march
4. max
5. wild
6. wild
7. November
8. October
9. September
20. wild

Unit 30   ABC Order   May 12, 2009

1. April
2. Aagust
3. blind
4. chilb
5. Deecember
6. February
7. frind
8. grind
9. Janyary
10. July
11. June
12. kind

(100)

Wendays

10-13-2011

The Zippity Zinger

Henry Winkler and

Lin Oliver

1. who is Hank Zipzer

The main chareter.

2. where does hank live

In an apartment b...

3. who doe Hank live with

Hank live with his,

mom and dad and his sister

Emily dog papa and

Katherine.

4. wgat city does Hank live in

Hank lives in new york city

5 what grade is Hank in

Hank is a fourth grade

grader.

Would you like to see your manuscript become a book?

If you are interested in becoming a PublishAmerica author, please submit your manuscript for possible publication to us at:

acquisitions@publishamerica.com

You may also mail in your manuscript to:

**PublishAmerica
PO Box 151
Frederick, MD 21705**

www.publishamerica.com

CPSIA information can be obtained at www.ICGtesting.com
Printed in the USA
LVOW061152020112

261890LV00001B/179/P